MW01119465

The Battle of Kursk: The History and Legacy of the Biggest Tank Battle of World War II

By Charles River Editors

A Panzer Unit at the Battle of Kursk

About Charles River Editors

Charles River Editors provides superior editing and original writing services across the digital publishing industry, with the expertise to create digital content for publishers across a vast range of subject matter. In addition to providing original digital content for third party publishers, we also republish civilization's greatest literary works, bringing them to new generations of readers via ebooks.

Sign up here to receive updates about free books as we publish them, and visit Our Kindle Author Page to browse today's free promotions and our most recently published Kindle titles.

Introduction

A Soviet machine gun in action at the battle

The Battle of Kursk

"The Russians have learnt a lot since 1941. They are no longer peasants with simple minds. They have learnt the art of war from us." – Wehrmacht Generaloberst Hermann "Papa" Hoth at Kursk (Healy, 1992, 90)

"On the German side, the reserves which will become so desperately necessary as the war situation develops […] will be tied down and thrown away uselessly. I consider the operation that has been planned a particularly grave error, for which we shall suffer later." – Colonel Reinhard Gehlen, Wehrmacht intelligence analyst, writing about Operation Citadel (Fowler, 2005, 66).

The vast expanses of southern Russia and the Ukraine provided the Eastern Front arena where the armies of Third Reich dictator Adolf Hitler and Soviet dictator Josef Stalin wrestled lethally for supremacy in 1943. Endless rolling plains – ideal "tank country" – vast forests, sprawling cities, and enormous tracts of agricultural land formed the environment over which millions of men and thousands of the era's most formidable military vehicles fought for their respective overlords and ideologies.

The winner could expect to reap very high stakes indeed. If Hitler's Wehrmacht smashed the Red Army, he could no longer hope for a lightning conquest, but the Fuhrer could expect the Soviet strongman to sue for peace on terms advantageous to Germany. If, conversely, the Red Army triumphed, Stalin could continue rallying the Soviet Union and move closer to expelling the loathed "Nemets" invaders from Russian soil – and perhaps carve out a Soviet empire in Central Europe.

Asserting that changes in the military leadership style of the two contending dictators explains the outcome of Kursk oversimplifies the actual situation. Logistics, the emergence of a body of experienced junior officers in the Red Army, American Lend-Lease shipments, German production problems, and other issues all contributed to the observed result.

However, the overarching factor tying everything together remained the changing approach of each leader to their army. At the start of the war, Hitler gave his commanders considerable initiative while Stalin fatally micromanaged his, and the Germans ripped vast hordes of Soviets to shreds with comparative ease. In late 1942 and moving into 1943, Hitler commenced micromanaging the Wehrmacht, and Stalin adopted a more "hands-off" approach permitting his commanders considerable initiative: "At the heart of the Red Army's lopsided tank losses was an amateurish and self-destructive style of decision imposed by Stalin [...] In November 1942 there was a subtle shift in the Red Army, as months of military disasters finally caused Stalin to reduce some of his interference [...] and allow quiet professionals such as Vasilevsky, Vatutin and Rokossovsky to prepare proper offensives." (Forczyk, 2013, 257).

Though the Wehrmacht remained too formidable and professional to collapse as readily as the appallingly low-quality Red Army had in 1941 and early 1942, the Red Army slowly got the upper hand and achieved strategic offensive momentum. That the shift occurred at the moment when Hitler hamstrung his generals with his melodramatic obstructionism while Stalin gave his some operational breathing room probably represents no accident.

Kursk represented the transitional battle during which the Red Army first demonstrated its new capabilities. The Soviets possessed better commanders than at the start of the war, a numerous soldiery, good-quality equipment (in particular, the T-34 tank), and the beginnings of a professional officer corps. Nevertheless, it required personal, ham-handed intervention by Adolf Hitler to transform Kursk from a probable hard-won Wehrmacht victory into a marginal but highly significant defeat.

The Battle of Kursk: The History and Legacy of the Biggest Tank Battle of World War II chronicles the crucial battle that became a turning point in Russia for both sides. Along with pictures of important people, places, and events, you will learn about Kursk like never before, in no time at all.

The Battle of Kursk: The History and Legacy of the Biggest Tank Battle of World War II

About Charles River Editors

Introduction

Chapter 1: Preparations for Operation Citadel

The military actions of previous years set up the conditions resulting in the Battle of Kursk in July 1943. Following the utter devastation wreaked on the unprepared Red Army in 1941 during Operation Barbarossa, the Germans encountered steadily increasing Soviet pressure. A sort of seesaw alternation of offensives ensued, in which the Germans went on the attack during the summer months and the Soviets counterattacked in winter.

Hitler's "Fall Blau" offensive in 1942 aimed to seize the Caucasus oil fields, but failed to do so. Instead, stripping the rest of the Wehrmacht lines of units led to the encirclement and destruction of the 6th Army at Stalingrad. The Soviets carried out a strong counteroffensive in southern Russia and the Ukraine during the winter of 1942-1943. The Red Army seized the city of Kharkov, then lost it again on March 14th, 1943.

Though the Wehrmacht eventually contained the Soviets, the attack created a massive salient centered on Kursk. A pause followed as the spring "Rasputitsa" – the Russian thaw, which turns dirt roads and fields alike into seas of sticky mud a yard deep or more – brought both armies to an effective halt.

The Kursk salient, jutting from Soviet into German territory, measured 74.5 by 118 miles, or around 8,700 square miles, approximately the same size as the entire U.S. state of New Jersey. Containing huge numbers of Soviet soldiers and tanks, it made an extremely tantalizing target for a battle of encirclement, such as those that devastated the Red Army in 1941 and to a lesser degree in 1942. If the Germans could "pinch off" the salient at the base, the Soviet war effort might suffer a sufficient blow for Stalin to seek peace.

The attack on the Kursk Salient – codenamed Operation "Zitadelle" or Citadel – also represented a slave raid on a giant scale. With serious manpower issues, the Germans needed slaves to increase factory production and make large numbers of the new, advanced tanks and aircraft their scientists developed. Hitler hoped Citadel would yield hordes of prisoners to man the Third Reich's factories.

The coming offensive provoked a surprising amount of argument in the high commands of both the Wehrmacht (OKW) and the Red Army (STAVKA). Stalin wanted another bold offensive, and Deputy Commander-in-Chief Marshal Georgi Zhukov and Chief of General Staff Marshal Aleksandr Vasilevsky found themselves called upon to muster all their courage and oppose their dictator's wishes. Zhukov declared:

> it will be better if we wear the enemy out in defensive action, destroy his tanks, and then, taking in fresh reserves, by going to an all-out offensive, we will finish off the enemy's main grouping (Healy, 1992, 10).

At the STAVKA meeting on April 12th, 1943, the two Marshals held their ground against Stalin – an act of considerable valor in itself. Where Hitler might demote a recalcitrant general in a fit of pique, Stalin ordered men shot or sent to labor camps for similar daring. However, the Soviet dictator listened, perhaps impressed by the two men's boldness. Zhukov also carefully wove promises of offensives into the chiefly defensive plan, and his own reputation for extreme aggression doubtless gave weight to his words.

Georgi Zhukov in 1941

Stalin also possessed intelligence from several foreign sources indicating German interest in attacking at Kursk. The German communist Rudolf Roessler, remaining out of Hitler's reach in Switzerland, obtained swift, accurate information on Wehrmacht decisions through his still-unknown OKW contacts, the "Lucy Ring," and passed them on to Stalin. The "Cambridge Five," including the infamous Kim Philby and the "Fifth Man" John Cairncross, confirmed this data with intelligence stolen from the British ULTRA program. Stalin disregarded this information until Zhukov confirmed it, however.

Stalin agreed to let the Soviet generals meet the Germans on the defensive, turning the Kursk salient into a gigantic fortress on which the Wehrmacht would hopefully dash itself to pieces. With their supreme leader's approval finally secured, the Soviet commanders set about their task with thoroughness and gusto.

The Soviets eventually committed ten armies to the Kursk region, though they did not deploy all of them immediately. The north flank of the salient, designated the Central Front, faced the German staging area and rail-head at Orel, and fell under the command of the tall, powerfully-built Marshal Konstantin Rokossovsky. The southern half of the salient, commanded by Marshal Nikolai Vatutin, bore the name of the Voronezh Front. The Soviets anchored the Voronezh Front on Oboyan and Prokhorovka – small points on the map soon to become immortally famous in history.

Nikolai Vatunin

Behind the two main fronts, to the east, lay the Steppe Front with reserve and counterattacking forces under the former lumberjack Ivan Konev, who established a formidable reputation for skilled military deception and who proved himself the equal in brutality of any Einsatzgruppen commander with his evident relish in massacring thousands of German POWs.

The Soviets set about building a triple layer of echeloned defenses around much of the Kursk salient's perimeter, featuring every kind of defensive work that time and resources permitted them to use. Anti-tank ditches, "Pakfronts" of dug-in anti-tank guns, barbed wire entanglements, bunkers, firing pits, and every other kind of prepared position soon formed a belt 30 miles deep around the salient's rim. The Red Army used not only its soldiers but approximately 300,000 drafted civilians and tens of thousands of POWs to build the defenses. Most of the civilian work crews consisted of women.

Guessing the heaviest Wehrmacht attacks would fall at the base of the salient in an effort to cut it off with a pincer movement, Vatutin and Rokossovsky built their strongest defenses there. Huge minefields covered much of the landscape, along with obstacles intended to channel the Germans into prepared kill zones. The Russians set up and preemptively sighted in vast concentrations of artillery on the most likely assault routes. The Red Army offered cash premiums of 200 to 1,500 rubles to men who actually knocked out Wehrmacht tanks, with the amount varying by method.

Since the Soviets planned immediate counterattacks once the Wehrmacht attack subsided, they also created a whole-new formation. This formation, the tank army, originated with General Pavel Rotmistrov, who presented the idea first to Lieutenant General Nikita Khrushchev, then to Stalin himself:

> I gave the tankers' opinion that it was necessary to organize and improve the mass employment of tanks, for which it was necessary to create tank armies of homogenous composition, and to reexamine their use on the battlefield. [...] Stalin received me and listened to me attentively. He then approved all my proposals. Several days later, the decision to create the 5th Guards Tank Army took place (Zamulin, 2010, 47).

Of course, formation of the tank armies on short notice proved difficult and some were filled out with obsolete early war Soviet tanks or with flimsy M3 Lee light tanks from America, known by the grim but clever nickname of "the Coffin for Seven Brothers." Each tank army needed approximately 5,000 trucks to support its mobility, including bringing up supplies of 600 tons of fuel daily. Without the tens of thousands of U.S. Lend-Lease trucks available to the USSR in 1943, Rotmistrov's tank armies would have proved impossible. Even with this aid, a severe shortage of trucks existed.

The M3 Lee

The tank armies took part in Kursk, particularly in the famous Battle of Prokhorovka. They also led the counter-punch once Operation Citadel foundered. The Germans also possessed formidable fortifications, including barbed wire, minefields, and improvised bunkers, designed to soak up the initial push of any Red Army attack and leave it prey to the mobile German divisions.

Chapter 2: The Germans Ready for Kursk

Hitler's anticipation of another offensive victory did not represent as far-fetched an expectation as it might appear. Though the Red Army's fighting and leadership qualities improved rapidly in late 1942 and into 1943, the Wehrmacht still repeatedly demonstrated its superiority and capacity to smash even extremely powerful Russian formations through use of maneuver and flexible, aggressive tactics.

Exactly one year prior, on July 5th, 1942, Zhukov launched an attack by 700 tanks near Orel, only to see his assault obliterated by the Germans in a huge tank battle that cost his forces 500 armored fighting vehicles. The indomitable Walther Model – who once made even Hitler quail with a frosty glare – crushed Operation Mars, a Soviet attack against the Rzhev Salient, in November 1942, encircling the Russian offensive forces and reducing no less than 1,800 of their 2,300 tanks to burning hulks.

Walter Model

In light of such triumphs, victory over an opponent who outnumbered the Germans just 1.3:1 in some areas and a maximum of 2:1 (in certain types of aircraft) in the Kursk Salient appeared plausible to the Fuhrer and some of his generals.

A number of experienced Wehrmacht commanders demurred, however. A see-saw debate continued through the first half of 1943 between Hitler and the generals who favored an offensive on one side, and those who opposed an attack on the other. Hitler's will obviously would prevail, but such excellent commanders as Heinz Guderian, Erich von Manstein, and Hans von Kluge continued to argue against the attack.

Heinz Guderian

Guderian, a famous panzer leader, suggested concentrating all available units into a single force and attacking just one side of the salient with maximum concentration of force. The northern side, supported by the rail-head at Orel, provided an obvious choice for this move. Erich von Manstein, an extremely capable general with a string of victories to his credit, preferred luring the Soviets out of their prepared positions in the Kursk Salient, and, once their offensive drove deep into German lines and overextended itself, pinching it off and wiping it out in detail.

Erich von Manstein

On April 15th, the Fuhrer proclaimed:

> This attack is of decisive importance. It must be a quick and conclusive success. It must give us the initiative for this spring and summer … Every officer, every soldier must be convinced of the decisive importance of this attack. The victory of Kursk must shine like a beacon to the world (Kershaw, 2009, 636).

Nevertheless, to the rising distress of even those generals in favor of it, the offensive suffered multiple postponements. Hitler moved the date from May to June and finally to an unspecified moment in July. The German defeat in North Africa made rapidity essential before American and British troops reached Europe. However, the Fuhrer wanted to wait until his engineers and factories finished a number of new fighting vehicles.

Hitler relied on the deployment of a several new and "secret" weapons systems to tip the scales in favor of the Wehrmacht. These included the formidable Panzer V Panther heavy tank, the Panzer VI Tiger, and the enormous Sd. Kfz. 184 Ferdinand, also dubbed the Elefant. The Brummbär infantry support gun, a massive self-propelled gun with a short-barreled 15cm howitzer for armament, also debuted during Citadel.

The performance of the Tigers in their first-ever action against Soviet T-34 tanks at Tomarovka on March 13th boosted German hopes for the new weapons system still higher, as Erhard Raus later recounted:

> our Tigers took up well-camouflaged positions and made full use of the longer range of their 88mm main guns. Within a short time they knocked out sixteen T-34s [...] and when the others turned about, the Tigers pursued the fleeing Russians and destroyed eighteen more tanks. Our 88mm armor-piercing shells had such a terrific impact that they ripped off the turrets of many T-34s and hurled them several yards. The German soldiers [...] immediately coined the phrase: "The T-34 tips its hat whenever it meets a Tiger" (Raus, 2005, 191).

Hitler dithered and delayed, which enabled a massive Soviet buildup in the Kursk Salient. Offsetting this advantage, the Wehrmacht also gained additional time to move men, materiel, and supplies into Operation Citadel's staging areas. Each unit shifted the region committed the Wehrmacht more irrevocably to a "showdown" near Kursk.

The Third Reich's supreme leader only decided on the exact date for Citadel's launch – July 5th, 1943 – on July 1st. Nevertheless, the excellence of Soviet spying ensured that Stalin, the STAVKA, and the field commanders knew this date within 24 hours of Hitler issuing his top-secret command, totally denying the Wehrmacht either strategic or tactical surprise. Though the Germans attempted to conceal the date – for example, by having Erich von Manstein participate in an award ceremony with the Romanian leader Ion Antonescu on July 3rd in Bucharest, then board his headquarters train surreptitiously and immediately journey towards the front – their deceptions failed completely.

Chapter 3: The Opposing Armies

The Germans and Soviets mustered the maximum number of men, tanks, other vehicles, and aircraft available for the battle of Kursk. Both the OKW and the STAVKA knew the encounter constituted the main and decisive action of summer 1943. Its outcome would determine the shape of the "Ostfront" conflict in 1944 also. Therefore, neither side held anything back when mustering their armies for the crisis.

Walther Model led the northern force, directed against Rokossovsky's Central Front. Model's force, the 9th Army, included 800 tanks, with only 45 Tigers. The Germans deployed the 83 available Elefant (Ferdinand) tank destroyers in this sector, supported by Brummbär self-propelled howitzers and Borgward IV radio-controlled demolition tanks.

A Group of German Soldiers at Kursk

Model received no Panzer V Panthers and his best tanks consisted of Panzer IV Ausf. H vehicles, outgunning the T-34s but slower due to their gasoline engines (as opposed to the vigorous diesel engine of the T-34). The 9th Army also included 196 Sturmgeschutz StuG Ausf. G self-propelled guns (SPGs) and 31 Sturmhaubitze StuH 42 self-propelled howitzers.

Air support for the 9th Army came from 686 combat aircraft of Luftflotte 6, including many excellent Focke Wulf Fw-190A fighters, commanded by Robert von Greim. Artillery support consisted of 3,630 tubes plus 165 of the infamous Nebelwerfer rocket launchers, variously dubbed the "Screaming Mimi," the "Howling Heinie," and the "Moaning Minnie." Though Model commanded 15 infantry divisions as part of the 9th Army, only eight of these saw action during Citadel. Total manpower in all branches stood at approximately 335,000 (Frankson, 2004, 18).

Rokossovsky, by contrast, deployed 711,575 men (both combat troops and non-combat support personnel) on the Central Front. His armored forces consisted of 1,785 tanks and self-propelled guns (SPGs). Of these, 456 comprised the 2nd Tank Army, led by Lieutenant General Aleksei Rodin. T-34/76s made up approximately 7 out of 10 of Rokossovsky's tanks, with the remainder T-70 light tanks, the latter practically useless against Panzer IIIs and IVs. Rokossovsky also had around 40 KV-1 heavy tanks.

Panzer III and Panzer IVs

The Soviets fielded a few SU-152 tank destroyers – the famous "Zveroboi" or "Beast Fighter," so called because it combated "Panthers" and "Tigers" – at Kursk. The most common SPG, however, consisted of the SU-76, a lightly-armored, open-topped tank destroyer known by a number of unflattering nicknames due to its vulnerability and the high lethality of serving in these machines. The Soviet soldiers called the SU-76 the "Suka," or "Bitch," as well as the "Golozhopy Ferdinand," or "Bare-Ass Ferdinand."

12,453 artillery tubes, anti-tank guns, and mortars supported the Central Front, together with 1,050 aircraft. Rokossovsky's force also mustered 41 rifle divisions, many of them close to their notional strength of 9,600 men apiece. These soldiers showed far higher morale and possessed much better equipment and training than the untrained and often unarmed unfortunates sent to their doom by Stalin in 1941 and early 1942.

In the south, Vatutin and his Voronezh Front found themselves pitted against Erich von Manstein and a stronger Wehrmacht force. Manstein's Army Group South

Luftflotte 4 supported Army Group South

Chapter 4: Initial Assault in the North

The first moves near Orel occurred after night fell on July 4th when thousands of German sappers crawled forward into the gigantic minefields guarding the approaches to the Central Front. Probing carefully at the ground and lifting out the mines they located to clear lanes through the extensive minefields, these men proved their outstanding professionalism by clearing one mine per minute per man for hours. By early morning on July 5th, they had prepared routes through the minefields for the attacking vehicles and infantry, marking these with short stakes and tape.

Zhukov, knowing the exact hour of the German deployment, ordered a preemptive artillery barrage on the suspected Wehrmacht mustering positions at 2:20 AM on the 5th. Thousands of guns opened fire, lighting up the sky with their muzzle flashes and shaking the earth with a furious, staccato barrage of explosions. The Soviet gunners hit almost no Germans, but managed to destroy almost all the stakes and route tape laid by the Wehrmacht sappers, erasing nearly every sign of the lanes through the minefields.

The intensity of Russian artillery fire, despite its poor aim, prompted Model to order a 2.5-hour delay in the attack while German artillery engaged in counterbattery fire. The Soviets' excellent artillery outranged that of the Wehrmacht, however, and only the frontline artillery batteries lay within reach of the Germans' lighter guns.

Accordingly, Luftflotte 6 sent forward their massed formations of medium bombers and Stuka dive-bombers to pound Russian defensive positions and batteries. Focke Wulf FW-190A fighters screened these vulnerable aircraft, and soon engaged an aggressive counterattack by the Soviet 16th Air Army.

Rather than enjoying full air superiority, the Germans found themselves plunged into an aerial struggle as ferocious and uncertain as the battle unfolding on the ground. Lieutenant General Sergei Rudenko botched the deployment of his brave pilots and their improved-quality aircraft by sending them in "penny packets" rather than immense formations, however. During 2,088 sorties, Luftflotte 6 shot down 100 Soviet aircraft (83 of them fighters) at a cost of 25 of their own aircraft (Forczyk, 2014, 49).

Model, a brilliant defensive general, proved himself somewhat less acute while on the offensive. Instead of a rapid *Schwerpunkt* with his panzers, followed up by mechanized infantry, the Third Reich general opened his attack with infantry on foot, deployed in sequential fashion that reduced their impact even further. The Soviet 13th Army fought back fiercely, while the Germans negotiated a landscape rendered deadly by the 503,000 anti-tank and anti-personnel mines the Soviets laid along the salient's northern face.

The 78th Assault Division led the attack, a unit at full strength and including many experienced veterans. The first 45 Elefant (Ferdinand) tank destroyers crawled forward in support, "brewing up" Soviet tanks with lethally accurate rounds from their long-barreled 88mm guns. The 78th Assault Division took heavy losses, however, and nearly found itself brought to a complete halt at Hill 257.7:

> Studded with bunkers supported by dug-in tanks, the Russian position was a nightmare version of the kinds of defenses Americans would encounter two years later on Okinawa. It quickly won the nickname "Panzer Hill" [...] The Ferdinands went forward anyway. Enough of them reached the defenses, and enough infantry managed to follow, that the hill fell to close assault—a polite euphemism for a series of vicious fights in which bayonets were civilized weapons (Showalter, 2013, 63).

The desperate struggle of the 78th Assault Division carried it forward only 3 miles by nightfall, a trivial distance compared to the number of miles to Kursk itself, the target of the drive. However, greater success attended the trio of panzer divisions and four infantry divisions Model sent towards the strongpoint of Ponyri. Led by Major General Mortimer von Kessel, the 20th Panzer Division blasted their way forward in the van, moving behind a rolling barrage of artillery fire. They took the town of Bobrik and extended the 9th Army's advance to five miles on the first day.

Nearby, the 45 Tiger tanks provided to 9th Army wreaked havoc out of proportion to their numbers, nearly succeeding in reaching the rear of the Soviet 81st Rifle Division and running amok there. The massive, boxy tanks engaged infantry, bunkers, and AT guns just as often as enemy tanks, using high explosive (HE) shells to deal with these threats.

In the case of towed anti-tank guns, the Tigers often conserved ammunition by simply running them over and crushing them under their treads. In some instances, Soviet infantry with no anti-tank weapons stood their ground against the steel giants with suicidal courage, achieving nothing except raising the levels of carnage higher, as a Tiger commander described:

> Red soldiers appeared in front of the tank. We drove directly into a defensive position. "Coax [i.e. 'coaxial machine-gun']!" The brown-clad figures rose in masses,

kneeling and standing, firing with their machine-pistols and rifles against our steel armor. A few pulled back. [...] They could not stop us. Those who were not cut   down by the bursts of our machine gun fire were run over (Lochmann, 2008, 144).

The Germans forced their way approximately five miles deep into Rokossovsky's Central Front on the first day of Operation Citadel, creating a salient 9 miles wide in the base of the Kursk Salient. This effort came at high cost, however, particularly to Model's already scarce infantry. As firefights and artillery bombardment continued throughout the night, the Germans retrieved and repaired as many damaged tanks and tank destroyers as possible, preparing for the renewed struggle on the next day.

Chapter 5: Counterattacks and the Battle for Ponyri

During the night, Rokossovsky decided to commit much of Rodin's 2nd Tank Army and the independent 19th Tank Corps to a counterattack early on July 6th. Motivated mainly by fear of his dictator – Rokossovsky "still remembered having his teeth smashed out by the NKVD while in prison and had no intention of giving Stalin a chance to condemn him for inactivity" (Forczyk, 2014, 51) – hectored Rodin into an ill-advised piecemeal attack against German panzers standing on the defensive.

Konstantin Rokossovsky

Hampered by their own infantry and defensive positions, the first elements of the 2nd

Tank Army finally approached Bobrik at 10:40 AM. The T-34s rolled forward across over a mile of open ground towards a village where dozens of Panzer VI Tiger tanks lurked. Under a light overcast with rain showers falling, the 107th Tank Brigade under Polkovnik Nikolai Teliakov advanced bravely towards the silent village.

Suddenly, the thunderous whipcrack sound of long-barreled 88mm tank guns ripped through the air. Tank after tank slewed to a halt, punctured by massive shells, torn apart from within by the orange blast of explosions, shedding tracks and turrets as the detonations tore them apart. In just three minutes, the Tiger gunners destroyed 45 of Teliakov's tanks at no loss on their side.

The 164th Tank Brigade, seeing Teliakov and his men slaughtered in a furious storm of shells, swung wide in an effort to avoid Bobrik and ran headlong into the 2nd Panzer Division. In the vicious fight that followed, the 164th lost 23 of its 50 tanks, but managed to destroy 10 Panzer IVs and tank destroyers before retreating.

Once the Luftwaffe once again drove Rudenko's luckless airmen from the immediate vicinity – destroying 91 Soviet fighters at a cost of 11 of their own – Model ordered the advance resumed on a six-mile front, advancing towards Ponyri. The day cleared around noon and the temperature soared into the upper 80s under a brilliant, baking sun. The tank crews drove with their hatches open for fresh air as the 2nd Panzer Division, the 20th Panzer Division, the 505th Tiger Battalion, and a number of infantry divisions pushed forward against the 2nd Tank Army and the defending Soviet infantry.

Ponyri, the goal of this push, remained out of reach on July 6th. Instead, a brutal struggle involving tens of thousands of men on each side developed as the Germans pushed relentlessly but gradually forward. Soviet and Wehrmacht tanks clashed, leading to rapidly mounting armor losses on both sides.

Curtains of artillery fell, and fighter-bombers and ground-attack aircraft, including the famous Shturmovik, hunted tanks and infantry concentrations amid the rolling folds of the plains, the burning villages, clumps of trees, and tall fields of rye. The two sides tore at each other with every weapons system available, from rifles and machine guns to Nebelwerfer and Katyushka rocket launchers to the heaviest artillery and bombs.

Over the next five days, the Germans pushed their way forward in brutal fighting until they finally reached Ponyri on the 10th and into the 11th. This "Stalingrad of the Steppes," as the combatants dubbed it, became the focus for extremely intense fighting for days. The Soviets distributed a pamphlet describing the life and heroic death of Konstantin Blinov, Hero of the Soviet Union, in bombastic terms to rouse their tank soldiers to fighting fury:

At Ponyri, Blinov did not leave the battlefield for three days. An expert soldier, he was sent to the most crucial points in our defenses. Wherever Blinov came with his tank, the enemy was sure to sustain a defeat. […] Blinov destroyed six enemy tanks, eight antitank guns and nine weapon emplacements; with machine gun fire and the treads of his tank, he killed 350 Germans (Fowler, 2005, 55).

The men of both sides exhibited heroic courage and endurance in what became a pounding, relentless battle of attrition. Thousands died and thousands more sustained wounds, necessitating their difficult evacuation from the battlefield when their comrades could rescue them. Though Model reached Ponyri, he could not push beyond it in the teeth of Soviet grit, determination, numbers, and lethal concentrations of artillery.

Reaching the town hollowed out 9th Army, inflicting 50,000 casualties on the Germans, the loss of 400 tanks, and the destruction of 500 aircraft. Though Soviet losses ranged higher, and Germans eventually retrieved and repaired many of their knocked out tanks to fight again, Model's 9th Army could do no more. The full extent of its achievement during Operation Citadel consisted of penetrating 10 miles into Soviet lines before further advance grew impossible.

Chapter 6: Attack of the Ferdinand or Elefant

A frequently underrated contribution to the attack of the 9th Army in the north came from the 83 "Ferdinand" Sd. Kfz. 184 heavy tank-destroyers of schwere Panzerjager-Abteilung 653 and schwere Panzerjager-Abteilung 654, better known to history by the name of "Elefant." These massive vehicles weighed in at 70 tons combat weight and consisted of a Tiger tank hull with a massive, boxy superstructure mounted at the rear.

A Disabled Elefant

With armor up to 7.87 inches thick (200mm), the Elefant provided a sort of moving fortress on the battlefield, capable of sustaining numerous hits from Russian tank guns from the frontal angle without being knocked out. Armament consisted of the long-barreled 8.8cm Pak 43/2 L/71, which combined the devastating hitting power of the 88mm German anti-tank gun with the long-range accuracy of a barrel 71 calibers long (hence the designation L/71). Elefant crews noted successful hits on some Russian tanks at ranges of 1.8 miles (3,000 meters) during the Kursk engagement.

Historians note the Elefant's slow speed (19 miles per hour at maximum in optimal conditions), tendency to mechanical problems, and relative vulnerability to Soviet anti-tank teams when unsupported by their own infantry due to the lack of an external machine gun. While correct, these criticisms ignore the immense combat power the Elefant demonstrated during the battle at Kursk.

When deployed during the battle, Borgward IV Schwerer Ladungstrager radio controlled demolition vehicles moved ahead of the Elefants to clear mines. These 3.5 ton remote-controlled vehicles cleared lanes through the thick Soviet minefields, and also knocked out some anti-tank gun positions. Unlike smaller radio controlled vehicles used by the Wehrmacht such as the

Goliath "beetle tank" tracked mine, the Borgward IV dropped its explosive charge and then moved away before detonation, enabling reuse.

42 Sturmpanzer Brummbär infantry support guns armed with short-barreled Skoda 15cm (6 inch) howitzers, organized into three squadrons of 14 Brummbär vehicles apiece, followed the advancing Elefant units. These massive, lumbering mobile artillery turrets fired indirectly over the Elefants to give them close-range heavy artillery support.

Unteroffizer J. Bohm expressed the qualified but widespread appreciation of Elefant crews for their massive, lumbering tank destroyers in a July 19th after-action report:

The main gun is very good. It destroys every tank with one or two rounds, even the KV II and the sloped American ones. [...] The Ferdinand has proved itself. They were decisive here, and we cannot go against the mass of enemy tanks today without a weapon of its type. [...] The engine is recognized as weak for the tonnage and the track is a bit narrow. If the vehicle is modified according to combat experiences, it will be fantastic! (Munch, 2005, 53).

Bohm recommended manufacturing 10 Elefants for every one then in service.

Out of the 83 Elefants engaged in combat at Kursk, the Russians destroyed only 13 (some demolished by their own crews when retrieval proved impossible). The Soviets knocked others out, and mines or engine fires disabled some, but the Germans retrieved all of these and put them rapidly back into service, in part thanks to their extremely rugged design. Due to their weight each Elefant required towing by 5 prime mover halftracks.

In exchange, the Elefants achieved 502 confirmed tank kills and destroyed approximately 200 anti-tank guns and 100 pieces of field artillery. The leading Elefants, directly engaged in combat, killed an average of 15 Soviet tanks apiece during Kursk, and one, under Lieutenant Heinrich Teriete, destroyed 22 tanks in just one day of combat, July 14th, 1943, winning the Lieutenant the prestigious Knight's Cross of the Iron Cross award.

Heinz Groschl, a Porsche engineer accompanying the units, reported on the Elefant's juggernaut indestructibility:

Hull – Has proved itself impervious to rounds. Except for one penetrating hit to the side near the rear ventilation motor housing (76 mm) and besides many scars, everything has remained intact. [...] Practical experience has shown however, that the engine gratings are a weak area. Apart from Molotov cocktails, a direct hit from artillery [...] on or near the gratings can set the vehicle ablaze (Munch, 2005, 55).

Far from being the "white elephant" portrayed by many historians, the Elefant proved utterly devastating in action against Soviet armor. Only its sluggish speed and limited numbers prevented it from exercising a more decisive role in Operation Citadel.

Chapter 7: Initial Assault in the South

Vatutin and Manstein squared off against each other along the Voronezh Front, where the Wehrmacht's Army Group South – including a number of elite SS armored divisions – prepared to land an even heavier blow against the Kursk Salient than Model launched in the north. A belt of approximately 440,000 mines, both anti-personnel and anti-tank, defended this face of the salient, behind which the Soviets manned their formidable triple defensive line.

One of the key anchors of the third, innermost line of defense lay at Prokhorovka Station, a railway stop near Skorovka. An insignificant stop on the rail line prior to 1943, military preparations transformed it into a linchpin of the defensive line. The Soviets placed a large supply depot and equally massive ammunition dump at Prokhorovka, supplying the 6th Guards Army. The railway made replenishment of these materiel stockpiles swift and efficient. The 2nd Air Army built a major airfield at Prokhorovka, while the 5th Guards Tank Army located its headquarters at Skorovka.

A formidable task confronted Manstein. Unlike the open "tank country" in the northern Kursk Salient, here natural defenses augmented the incredible maze of earthworks, tank traps, and dugouts created by the Soviets. Relatively common terrain features included woodland, tracts of ravines and broken ground, small rivers, swamps, marshes, many villages, and a number of farms.

Nevertheless, Vatutin's headquarters identified 13 viable attack routes for Manstein's heavy armor. Knowing of the SS units massed opposite them, Lieutenant General Mikhail Chistyakov, commander of the 6th Guards Army, exhorted his men immediately before the forces clashed, referring to them by the Soviet appellation of "Guards" units:

In front of you stand Hitler's Guards formations. We must expect the main effort of the German offensive on this sector (Fowler, 2005, 59).

On July 4th, 1943, elements of the Fourth Panzer Army advanced at 3 PM and took several hilltops that provided essential artillery observation posts. The main attack came some 12 hours later, beginning at 3 AM on July 5th and involving the advance of Army Group South's large force of panzers. The army deployed over 100 Tigers and 200 Panzer V Panthers, along with hundreds of Panzer IVs, most upgunned and fitted with armored skirts to provide extra protection to their vulnerable tracks.

The day came clear and with the promise of intense heat, though violent thunderstorms overnight generated more of the omnipresent mud that bedeviled both armies on the Eastern Front. The first move came in the air and developed thanks to an effort by the 2nd and 17th Soviet Air Armies to seize the initiative.

Large squadrons of Soviet Yak-3 an Ilyushin Il-2 fighters arrived at 4:20 AM, escorting 150 Shturmovik ground attack aircraft and several detachments of bombers. The Soviets hoped to catch the Luftwaffe still on their airfields, where the Shturmoviks could strafe them with their automatic cannons and the bombers destroy the Stukas and other aircraft, besides pitting the airstrips with craters.

The Germans, however, showed themselves alert and extremely active. The signals intelligence crews picked up a sudden spike in radio transmissions from the identified Soviet Air Army communications centers, and immediately telephoned the airfields. Even before long-range German radar detected the signatures of the incoming aircraft, ground crews pushed Stukas and bombers hastily off the sides of the rough airstrips and rolled out Messerschmitt Bf-109 and Focke-Wulf Fw-110A fighters to counter the challenge.

So swiftly did the highly professional crews and pilots work that by the time the incoming Soviet formations arrived, the German fighters already circled high in the sky, waiting for their prey. The Russians flew in low, expecting to strafe and bomb the airfields from a low altitude for maximum effect. The experienced Luftwaffe pilots dove against them like stooping hawks, taking the surprise attack by surprise. Soon, Soviet wrecks littered the landscape, and the rest fell back in the face of stinging German assaults.

No sooner had the Luftwaffe fighters chased off the Soviet incursion than 400 Stuka dive-bombers and medium tactical bombers swept forward to hammer the Soviets' prepared positions ahead of the panzer assault. The men of the 6th Guards Army held their ground with grim doughtiness as German bombs rained down and the Stukas descended again and again, their wing sirens shrieking as they plunged to deliver their lethal payloads on Russian artillery and antitank positions.

Behind the front lines, General Mikhail Chistyakov ensconced himself in the small apple orchard of a farm, expecting the German attack to shatter on the first line of defenses. General Mikhail Katukov, twice named Hero of the Soviet Union, and his aide Lieutenant General Nikolai Kirillovich Popel, arrived to inform him that, instead, Army Group South's elite SS armored units were breaking through the first line of entrenchments and that Chistyakov's al fresco headquarters lay in their path. As Popel later wrote:

On the table were cold mutton, scrambled eggs, a carafe with chilled vodka to judge by the condensation on the glass, and finely sliced white bread – Chistyakov was doing himself well (Fowler, 2005, 77).

In this manner, Chistyakov first learned from his less complacent subordinates that the heavy panzer attacks succeeded in punching through the Voronezh Front's outer boundary despite the frenzied efforts of the Russian soldiery to repel them.

Even the mighty panzer formations might have failed against the intricately interlocking trenches, bunkers, obstacles, tank traps, and antitank gun positions if not for the steady, accurate airstrikes provided by hundreds of Stukas. Junkers Ju 87G-1 and Henschel Hs 108B ground attack aircraft, armed with paired 37mm cannons, stalked the field, attacking Soviet armored units moving up to support the infantry lines.

Manstein tasked Army Group Kempf with driving through the Soviet lines on the right of the attack, guarding the eastern flank of the advance from counterattack. General Hermann Breith commanded this large detachment, which consisted of the 6th, 7th, and 19th Panzer Divisions, plus Heavy Panzer Battalion 503 containing Tigers and three battalions StuG III Sturmgeschutz self-propelled assault guns. Altogether, this force consisted of 300 Panzer VI, III, and a handful of Panzer II tanks and "Flammpanzer" flamethrower tanks, augmented by 45 Tigers and 75 StuG IIIs.

Delivery of the main *Schwerpunkt* fell to the responsibility of the 4th Panzer Army, commanded by Generaloberst Hermann Hoth. The 4th Panzer Army consisted of two Panzer Corps. The II SS Panzer Corps, led by the highly professional SS-Obergruppenfuhrer Paul Hausser, contained three elite SS-Panzergrenadier Divisions, *Leibstandarte Adolf Hitler*, *Das Reich*, and *Totenkopf*. These amounted to 327 tanks and 95 assault guns, including StuG IIIs and Hummels.

Paul Hausser

The other half of 4th Panzer Army, deployed on the left, comprised the XLVIII Panzer Corps, led by General Otto von Knobelsdorff. One of the regular Wehrmacht's finest divisions, the *Grossdeutschland* Panzergrenadier Division, formed the core of this formidable unit, and included 45 Tigers, 200 Panthers, and 120 Panzer IVs and Panzer IIIs in its roster, while commanded by a man with the resounding name of Hyazinth Graf Strachwitz von Gross-Zauche und Camminetz. The 3rd and 11th Panzer Divisions and the 167th Infantry Division rounded out the XLVIII Panzer Corps, which mustered 450 tanks and 45 assault guns overall (Nipe, 2012, 47-49).

Army Group South's strategic reserve consisted of three seasoned divisions, the SS-Panzergrenadier *Wiking* Division together with the 17th and 23rd Panzer Divisions.

The advancing German forces met ferocious, almost fanatical, resistance from the Soviets, a far cry from the panicked levies of the first years. The XLVIII Panzer Corps slogged forward in an endless series of hard-fought battles for the next section of trenches and bunkers, pushing 3 miles into Soviet lines on the first day.

The 3rd Panzer Division seized the fortified town of Korovino on the extreme left.

Meanwhile, *Grossdeutschland* and the 11th Panzer Division cooperated to attack Cherkassoye. Brave anti-tank squads of Soviets attempted to scramble up on the panzers and destroy them by attacking antitank mines to their turrets; some succeeded. The Wehrmacht finally dislodged Cherkassoye's valiant defenders through use of flamethrower tanks, whose ghastly effectiveness seared itself into the minds of the Germans also:

> A flamethrower crewman from Das Reich wrote of the "strange feeling to serve this destructive weapon and it was terrifying to see the flames eat their way forward and envelop the Russian defenders." A more matter-of-fact veteran of the day mentioned [...] in passing that ever since then he had been unable to tolerate the smell of roast pork (Showalter, 2013, 80).

The Soviets managed only localized counterattacks on July 5th, which the Wehrmacht also rolled up as they continued to press slowly forward. However, on July 6th, the Soviets moved up additional rifle battalions and tank brigades in larger counterstrikes against the still-advancing Wehrmacht. The Panzers continued to roll forward towards their next objective of Oboyan, fighting against the usual complex of defenses.

The Germans encountered General Mikhail Katukov's 1st Tank Army, having pushed clean through the 6th Guards Army. Many of Katukov's tanks occupied dug-in positions, despite the protests of his political officer, Nikita Khrushchev. However, a number of Katukov's vehicles also remained mobile, and at around noon, he threw these forward in a spoiling attack against the *Leibstandarte Adolf Hitler* Division.

Mikhail Katukov

The *Leibstandarte*'s Tiger detachment met the Soviet vehicles in a head-on encounter near Yakovlevo, where the II SS Panzer Corps had now pierced no less than 20 miles into the salient, a menacing development the Soviets could not ignore. One of the *Leibstandarte* tank commanders later described the action:

On separate slopes, some 1,000 meters apart, the forces faced one another like figures on a chess board […] They rolled ahead a few meters, pulled left, pulled right, maneuvered to escape the enemy crosshairs and bring the enemy into their own fire. […] After one hour, 12 T-34s were in flames. The other 30 curved wildly back and forth, firing as rapidly as their barrels would deliver. They aimed well but our armor was very strong. We no longer twitched when a steely finger knocked on our walls (Fowler, 2005, 83-85).

The armored spearheads of Manstein's advance pushed forward with the Tigers in the fore, Panthers and upgunned Panzer IVs guarding the flanks, and less well armored tanks following in support. Nikolai Popel expressed astonishment at the sheer numbers of German vehicles. Though the Russians fought desperately, the Tigers and other Wehrmacht tanks caved in the 1st Tank Army and continued their advance.

Behind the lines, repair crews worked ceaselessly to retrieve knocked out or broken down panzers, repair them, and send them back into action. Most hits temporarily disabled a vehicle rather than annihilating it; even after the Kursk action concluded, permanent losses and write-offs remained a surprisingly small item.

Katukov himself remained unconvinced of the value of armored counterattack, though the remote but hovering presence of Stalin, always questioning why his commanders did not immediately go on the offensive, encouraged these reckless actions anyway. Katukov later wrote:

> Let the fascists come crawling forward in the hope that at any moment, they'll succeed in breaking out into operational space. Let the Hitlerites get enmeshed in our defenses and die. We, in the meantime, will be grinding down the enemy's materiel and manpower. Once we bleed their units white and smash the fascists' armored fist, then the suitable moment will ripen for launching a mighty counterattack (Zamulin, 2010, 114).

The Germans fully broke through the first of the three Soviet lines of defense and pierced the second at one location by the end of July 6th. The Wehrmacht forces continued to push forward steadily on July 7th, 8th, and 9th, despite increasingly large and desperate counterattacks by the Soviets. Progress naturally slowed considerably for the Germans, and some of the commanders began to wonder if withdrawal represented the best option.

For his part, Vatutin committed every unit available to prevent a breakthrough into the "operational space" behind his three lines of defense. He knew clearly that once the Germans reached this relatively undefended ground, they could cut off hundreds of thousands of Soviet soldiers from their lines of supply and force their surrender. The Wehrmacht had already taken copious amounts of prisoners, but if the whole Kursk Salient fell, the Red Army's capacity to undertake offense action would likely vanish for the rest of the year, quite possibly forcing Stalin to sue for peace.

Army Group Kempf, meanwhile, had established a defensive line along the east of the German advance. There, as Theodor Busse, a German infantry general on Manstein's staff, remarked, they "stood like a rock wall" (Newton, 2002, 20), defending the tree belt along Koren Creek against Soviet counterattacks. In addition to using this natural strongpoint for defense, the Kempf group also managed to throw several bridgeheads across the Donets river, which might prove useful for later advances.

Though the Wehrmacht continued to advance and push against the second defensive line, their fighting strength slowly frayed. Damage to tanks and the loss of men took their toll on the army's ability to maintain operations over the longer term. Nevertheless, the Germans continued their efforts with consummate professionalism and steely determination – a resolve matched fully by their Soviet opponents.

The German offensive stalled on July 9th, leading to a conference among the leading German commanders. Hermann Hoth recommended a fresh assault, and Manstein supported him provisionally. Once he visited the frontline units personally and observed conditions for himself, Manstein gave Hoth approval for his renewed offensive.

Hermann Hoth

The 4th Panzer Army resumed its attack on July 11th and finally punched through the stubborn defenses that halted it two days before. The *Totenkopf* Division successfully crossed the Psel River on pontoon bridges, penetrating this stubbornly held line of defense. Other breakthroughs occurred, and this laid the groundwork for the most famous moment of the entire Battle of the Kursk Salient.

Late on July 11th, the II SS Panzer Corps under SS Obergruppenfuhrer Paul Hausser – a long-faced Prussian officer and SS fanatic who survived the war and lived until 1972 – moved forward to take up positions to attack Prokhorovka Station. Hausser deployed *Das Reich* on the right of his formation, *Liebstandarte* in the center, and *Totenkopf* on the left. At this moment, Vatutin decided to commit the entire 5th Guards Tank Army in an effort to halt the relentless German advance, now poised for a fatal breakthrough.

Chapter 8: The Battle of Prokhorovka

The Battle of Prokhorovka on July 12th, 1943, taking place near Prokhorovka Station, developed naturally out of the sequence of events leading up to it. Several frequent historical assertions about this battle constitute little more than mythology, though many historians continue to quote them. The research of post-Soviet Russian historians and the rediscovery of accounts by German generals and SS panzer leaders, however, paint a very different picture from the accepted view.

One myth states the Battle of Prokhorovka represented the biggest tank battle in history in terms of the number of vehicles engaged. While massive, several other battles actually involved more tanks, including the abortive Operation Mars in 1942 against the Rzhev Salient. Prokhorovka certainly stands among the top five largest tank encounters of world history, but is at best the second largest and perhaps the third or fourth.

The other myth is that the Soviets won an overwhelming victory and wiped out the German panzers at Prokhorovka. In fact, this springs from a false picture presented to Stalin by Red Army commanders seeking to prevent their own execution. In reality, though damaged by the massive, courageous Soviet attacks, Manstein's panzer formations decimated the 5th Guards Tank Army and its supporting units, then continued advancing through July 17th, pushing forward and achieving the position necessary for a decisive breakthrough, prevented only by Hitler's decisions.

The Soviet commander Vatutin viewed the situation with understandable alarm on July 11th, 1943. On July 9th, it appeared the Wehrmacht thrust finally exhausted its momentum in the second defensive line. But on July 10th, and even more strongly on July 11th, the Third Reich juggernaut rolled forward again, breaking through defensive lines and crushing the local counterattacks sent against it.

German Advancement towards Prokhorovka on July 11th.

Nikolai Vatutin – a capable man of high professionalism who inspired loyalty in his subordinates through his thoughtfulness and high regard for them, but who earlier suffered arrest, persecution, and extraction of several teeth in a Soviet dungeon – listened to a report from Pavel Alekseyevich regarding the fighting power of German armor and suggested tactics to counter it:

'The fact is that the Tigers and Ferdinands not only have strong frontal armor, but also a powerful, long-range direct fire 88mm gun. In that regard they are superior to   our   tanks, which are armed with 76mm guns. Successful struggle with them is only   possible   in circumstances of close-in combat, with exploitation of the T-34's greater maneuverability and by flanking fire against the side armor of the heavy German machines.' 'In other words, engage in hand-to-hand fighting and take them by boarding,' the *front* commander said (Zamulin, 2010, 268).

These tactics formed the basis for much of the later myth about Prokhorovka, but it remains one thing to propose tactics and another to successfully execute them. Nevertheless, Vatutin had little choice. The rail-head at Prokhorovka supplied many of his forces with ammunition, fuel, and food, making it a choice target for the Germans in any case. He also wanted to save the Soviet 48th Rifle Corps, in imminent danger of finding itself encircled and destroyed by the II SS Panzer Corps.

Above all, perhaps, he received dark hints by telephone from Stalin about retribution visited on parties unknown if the Germans reached the rear in the Prokhorovka area. Vatutin and his fellow commanders might experience a "nine-gram pension" – that is, be shot in the base of the skull – if the Wehrmacht broke through.

The 5th Guards Tank Army, and several other tank battalions Vatutin and Lieutenant General Rotmistrov managed to collect, moved forward and prepared for action to the north of Prokhorovka on July 11th. Part of the myth about the battle states that the Soviets managed complete surprise against the II SS Panzer Corps on July 12th. However, documentary evidence demolishes this view. The Germans did not stumble suddenly on the Soviet force; rather, they rapidly gained clear awareness of the Soviet preparations and stood on the defensive to receive the counterattack, a completely correct tactical response playing to the strengths of the Tigers and Panzer IVs against the T-34/76s.

An impossible task in an era of reconnaissance aircraft, assembling nearly 900 tanks and assault guns took many hours and could not be hidden in the rolling farmland near Prokhorovka. Besides aerial scouting, the men of *Leibstandarte* heard the roar of numerous tank engines in the early morning and carried out a brief but useful probing attack in the direction of the Soviet lines, which confirmed the buildup of heavy armor concentrations.

The Soviets attempted artillery support for their attack, which provided additional warning to the Germans but, for once, proved too haphazard to inflict much damage. The attached artillery of *Leibstandarte,* by contrast, inflicted considerable harm on the Russians. Worse, the Ju-87 Stukas, upgraded with a pair of 37mm cannons for tank busting, soon crisscrossed the skies, accompanied by bombers. Hans Rudel, the famous Stuka ace, tore into the advancing Soviet armor columns with gusto:

"The first flight flies behind me in the only cannon-carrying airplane.... In the first attack four tanks exploded under the hammer of my cannons; by the evening the total rises to twelve. We are all seized with a kind of passion for the chase...." (Showalter, 2013,

151).

Unleashed by the radio code phrase "Steel! Steel! Steel!," the entire 5th Guards Tank Army rolled forward at full speed towards and past Prokhorovka. Violet smoke erupted all along the line as the Germans fired their purple smoke shells, a color-coded signal indicating a tank attack. The crews ran to their vehicles and took up final fighting positions, choosing the military crest of long slopes where possible to give them a clear field of fire and good lines of sight. The Tiger crews, experienced men almost to a man, parked their Tigers at a slant so that the angled front armor presented an even greater thickness to the T-34 shells and caused most to harmlessly carome off even at point-blank range.

As the Soviets charged full-throttle across several miles of open ground, the Tigers and Panzer IVs began a terrible, methodical harvest of machines and men. Shell after shell screamed through the air to rupture hulls, set engines on fire, blow turrets off, and reduce human flesh to charred paste. Despite this lethal storm, the T-34s came on, followed by T-60 light tanks and SU-76 "Golozhopiy Ferdinand" assault guns.

SS-Obersturmfuhrer Rudolf von Ribbentrop (still alive as of New Year's 2016) led a section of 7 Panzer IVs in defense of a shallow valley. Positioning his tanks just below the top of a long slope overlooking a Soviet anti-tank ditch with a single bridge across it, Ribbentrop hammered the swarms of Soviet tanks with his vehicle's 75mm high velocity gun, while the other vehicles did the same. The densely packed T-34s crashed into the ditch in their effort to advance, and even after crossing the bridge, fared little better:

Burning T-34s drove into and over one another. It was a total inferno of fire and   smoke, and impacting shells and explosions. T-34s blazed, while the wounded tried   to crawl away to the sides. The entire slope was soon littered with burning enemy   tanks. We remained behind the smoldering wreck. Just then I heard my loader   report: "No   more   armor-piercing available!" (Kurowski, 2002, 197).

All along the line, the merciless scene repeated itself. Under an overcast sky (giving place later to thunderstorms) the Germans pounded Vatutin's tank force and its reserves to pieces. At one place, the Germans surrounded 93 T-34s and destroyed them all. After the battle, Hausser attempted to count them, lost track, and finally achieved a total by scrambling amid the giant steel carcasses with chalk, writing large numerals on each tank to reach a total.

Many of the T-34 tanks carried spare, unarmored fuel containers on their exterior. While this helped them achieve greater range, it also made them a species of rolling incendiary bomb, dangerous to neighboring vehicles and extremely fatal to their crews. Usually, tank crews needed to use an armor piercing (AP) round against an enemy tank to destroy it. However, the Germans soon discovered they could use high explosive (HE) rounds against the T-34s successfully, thus effectively increasing their onboard supply of anti-tank rounds. An HE hit on the fuel set it afire and destroyed the tank as surely as though it fell victim to a huge Molotov cocktail. In at least one case, this flammability led to a spectacular event commemorated by both sides.

A trio of Tigers, including those of Tiger ace Michael Wittman and that of Georg Lotzsch, engaged and destroyed 18 T-34s on one flank of *Leibstandarte*. After knocking out most of the tanks, Wittmann and Lotzsch witnessed three Russians emerge from a burning T-34 tank, two of them carrying a badly wounded friend. The two men hurried to a shell crater and placed the injured man in it for protection, while the Germans held their fire. Then, to the astonishment of the SS tank crews, the two Soviet tank crewmen climbed back into their holed and burning T-34/76. A moment later, it lurched forward directly towards Lotzsch's Tiger. Lotzsch

ordered an advance, to get clear of the smoke. The gunner fired—and the shell bounced off. The Russian kept coming and rammed the Tiger. As flames covered both tanks, the German suddenly backed up. At five yards' distance, the T-34 exploded (Showalter, 2013, 154).

Lotzsch's tank suffered only cosmetic damage from the explosion and immediately rejoined the fight, but the unknown, heroic Soviet crewmen entered legend. In an embellishment on the sober if surprisingly sympathetic German account, the Soviets claimed both tanks detonated in a rather cinematic fireball when the T-34 rammed the massive 45-ton Tiger.

Later Soviet accounts of the battle portray the T-34s boldly dashing into close contact with the surprised German tanks and destroying them en masse, though at considerable cost to themselves. The historicity of the Soviet triumphalist propaganda is clearly disproved by a few facts. The Soviets claimed they destroyed 400 German tanks – but the actual total tank strength of the II SS Panzer Corps on the day of battle numbered 211, with around 100 more undergoing repair far behind the front lines. They also claimed the destruction of 70-100 Tiger tanks, yet in fact the German force had only 15 Tigers on the day of Prokhorovka, none of which suffered destruction.

The muster reports of the two sides' tank units, paradoxically only studied by historians some 60 to 70 years after the battle, provide a much better picture of the outcome. These indicate German losses of approximately 70 tanks, most of which proved capable of repair. This still represents around a third of the Wehrmacht vehicles involved, and shows the desperation of the fighting and the determination of the outmatched Russians to come to grips and defeat their enemies.

On the Soviet side, Red Army documents show a stunning drop of 650 tanks in the 5th Guards Tank Army by July 13th. Of these, the Soviets eventually retrieved and repaired approximately 400. However, with the Germans left in possession of the battlefield, repair only occurred after the Germans later retreated for other reasons. For all practical purposes, the 5th

Guards Tank Army's roster fell from 800 to 150 tanks during the Prokhorovka fight.

The German General Theodor Busse provided a succinct summary of the situation in describing the battle, and also noted the continued advance, which only ended after July 17th when Hitler called off the offensive:

Fourth Panzer Army repulsed all attacks on 12-13 July without losing a foot of ground. For Army Group South, 14 July brought complete success along the entire front, and the enemy's offensive power appeared to have been broken. The requirements for cleaning out the southern bank of the Psel from Prokhorovka to a point north of Peny had been established. Pertinent orders for this operation had been issued (Newton, 2002, 24).

The Battle of Prokhorovka, in fact, represented a rather costly German victory. The courage, grit, and determination of the Red Army tankers remains undeniable. They gave their utmost and succeeded in inflicting relatively heavy losses on the elite SS tank units despite the enormous disadvantages they fought under. The Germans, of course, showed equal courage, great skill, and enjoyed the use of notably superior fighting machines.

In the end, the famous Battle of Prokhorovka differed only somewhat from the fight at Bobrik. The T-34/76 crews found themselves forced to attack over open country against adversaries whose tank guns could easily knock them out over a mile away, while their own guns only proved effective at ranges of 80 yards or less. Their only option involved racing forward as quickly as possible, trying desperately to close the distance, while continuing to fire in the hope of an extremely lucky shot.

The Germans, in a highly professional manner, stood on the defensive once they realized the Soviets targeted them with a major tank attack. Their seasoned SS gunners picked their targets and fired accurately, destroying tank after tank. The upgunned Panzer IVs proved deadly also, though more vulnerable to Soviet 76mm guns. Their long-barreled high-velocity 75mm cannons threw their shells with much greater velocity and accuracy than the short-barreled 76mm guns on the Soviet tanks.

Prokhorovka, in fact, generated enough accurate reports despite the myths forged for public consumption that the Soviets immediately began an improvement program to redesign the T-34. The resulting T-34/85, armed with an 85mm gun, outmatched Panzer IVs and could destroy Panthers and Tigers, though the two heaviest German tanks remained notably superior to all T-34 models in both firepower and protection.

Chapter 9: Late Stages of Citadel

At the same time that Army Group South's elite Panzergrenadier units fought the Battle of Prokhorovka, events unfolded elsewhere rendering their hard-won victory moot. With the 9th

Army brought to a halt against the Central Front due to lack of sufficient panzers, the Soviets loosed a counterattack towards Orel on July 12th under the operational name Operation Kutusov.

The offensive involved three Soviet armies – the 3rd and 63rd Armies under Colonel-General Markian Popov, detached from the Briansk Front, and the 11th Guards Army from the Western Front under General Vasily Sokolovsky.

Popov's offensive proved amateurish and blundering in the extreme. Directed at German defensive belts held by the 56th and 262nd Infantry Divisions, the luckless Soviet soldiers found themselves sent directly ahead into minefields, barbed wire entanglements, and defensive positions with interlocking fields of fire. Receiving almost no tactical direction whatever from their commander, the Russians suffered heavy losses and pushed forward only three miles before being brought to a halt.

Sokolovsky's 11th Guards Army attack represented a very different matter. This aggressively led force struck a sector commanded by the incompetent Generaloberst Ernst Fackenstedt, whose 5th Panzer Division lost 55 of its 100 Panzers permanently (as against *Leibstandarte's* permanent loss of just 7 tanks at Prokhorovka).

On July 13th, Walther Model in the north began withdrawing all units of the 9th Army from the modest 10-mile incursion they drove into Soviet lines. With Soviet counterattacks threatening Orel and the lifeline of its railway, Model needed all his troops to fend off the risk of encirclement. He reported:

"Already today it can be concluded from the scale of the offensive against 2. Panzerarmee that the enemy has set as his aim the complete conquest of the Orel Salient... radical changes have taken place during the last forty-eight hours. [...] The center of gravity of all operations has shifted to the panzer army. Here the crisis has continued to develop at unprecedented speed" (Nipe, 2012, 51).

Model managed to extricate most of his men from the potential trap, and joined his forces with those already in place opposing the Soviet advance. During the next two weeks, the Soviets slowly forced the Germans back, taking considerable losses in the process. The Elefant or Ferdinand tank destroyers proved even more lethal on the defense than on the attack in the open country where the combat occurred. Eventually, however, the Germans packed them on to trains and sent them elsewhere for refitting, before deploying some to other areas of Russia and some to Italy to fight the newly landed American and British allies.

Despite this northern counterattack, Manstein believed his Army Group South remained poised for a decisive breakthrough. While *Leibstandarte* withdrew somewhat to be refitted, repaired, and rearmed, and the men received a much needed rest period after the immense stress of a week of lethal combat, *Das Reich* and *Totenkopf* continued to press forward, taking river crossings and tactically valuable hills in preparation for an expanded offensive into the soft interior of the Kursk Salient.

Manstein asked Hitler to release the three Panzer Divisions held in reserve for Army Group South, intending to use them to break through and attain yet another stunning victory over the Red Army. His men already held 24,000 prisoners, the largest number taken for over a year in a single action. During the first week of the offensive, the Soviets lost tanks at a rate of approximately 10 vehicles destroyed for every 1 lost by the Germans. Manstein's notion of a larger strategic victory may not have been a mere pipe dream.

Nevertheless, Hitler refused to release the Panzer Divisions, squandering all the effort and sacrifice put into carrying out his Kursk attack by his hard-fighting German soldiery. Allied landings in Sicily on the night of July 9th to 10th opened Operation Husky, threatening the Italian mainland and opening a second front on the Eurasian continent. British deceptions cleverly misled Hitler into suspected an imminent Balkans landing also.

Faced by this situation, Hitler ordered the Kursk offensive halted and some of the divisions transferred west for refitting and redeployment against the Americans and British. The crucial meeting occurred on July 13th, when Hitler convened several of his commanders, including Manstein, at his "Wolf's Lair" or Wolfsschanze in the Masurian Forest of East Prussia (Poland).

Hitler employed his usual technique of letting his generals argue to an impasse and then stepped in to resolve the situation. The attack would be called off, though he allowed Manstein to pursue a few local objectives first, and several of the best divisions would be transferred to the Balkans – where the Fuhrer expected an attack that nevertheless never materialized – and the rest would go to Italy. The final German offensive on the Eastern Front reached its end with a few words from the Third Reich's supreme leader.

Chapter 10: Outcomes of the Battle of Kursk

Though the Battle of Kursk represented the first major Soviet victory on the Eastern Front for some time, it left the German army largely intact as a fighting force. The Wehrmacht retained its cohesion despite its personnel losses. The Germans retrieved most tanks damaged or knocked out in Kursk, repaired them, and returned them to action. Only the most shattered found no further use – the mechanics cannibalized the worse cases for parts to repair other tanks of similar make.

However, Kursk proved a highly important watershed. The battle presented the last strategic offensive by the Wehrmacht during the war, and stood as the turning point at which initiative changed irrevocably to the Soviets. The Red Army remained on the offensive for the rest of the war. Though Model, "the Fuhrer's Fireman," defeated individual offensives time and again, the Wehrmacht lost ground rapidly and steadily as the Soviet titan ground forward.

Soviet soldiers continued to show great bravery and developed moderate fighting skills as the war continued. Their officer corps grew more professional, operating as much as possible in a professional manner. However, Stalin remained something of a burden on his subordinates. He eschewed encirclements, as the first of these failed to achieve what he hoped for.

Rather than realizing the Red Army would improve with practice, he insisted on frontal assaults in all circumstances and at all times, preferring a febrile "patriotic" zeal to maneuver and scientific warfare. This, of course, cost the Soviets millions of additional dead, as the Germans tore at the Soviet "human waves" with the ferocity of a wounded predator. Nevertheless, the Soviets used tactics at a local level whenever possible, as their junior officers learned by experience.

Much of the explanation for the German failure at Kursk lies with the sheer numbers of Soviet soldiers, tanks, aircraft, and artillery involved. The Soviets prepared the Salient as a trap for the Germans with a colossal amount of human ingenuity and effort. The thirty mile deep defensive lines around the salient's boundaries proved sufficient to soak up the Wehrmacht's efforts.

A German Soldier's Grave at Kursk

In the north, where Kluge and Model lacked enough tanks, the Citadel attack failed to penetrate very far into the prickly, lethal thickets of the salient's defenses. The massed panzers in the south punched much deeper into the defensive belts and nearly broke through, though still at heavy cost. Infantry support also proved lacking. With not enough infantry, the Wehrmacht found themselves forced to use tanks to hold positions and guard flanks, eroding the Schwerpunkt's offensive drive even exclusive of casualties.

One possibly critical factor seldom explored in histories of Kursk involved the respective engine designs of Wehrmacht and Red Army tanks. Stalin, in a rare flash of insight, ordered his designers to produce only tanks with diesel engines. While Hitler manifested a brief flirtation with diesel during the early war years, he allowed the factory engineers to talk him out of its implementation:

Hitler expressed interest in developing a diesel tank engine – which he recognized offered savings in fuel and improved range – but German engineers fobbed off such ideas as 'too difficult and too time consuming,' so it was allowed to slide. If any   word describes the state of German tank design at the start of Barbarossa, it is   mediocrity (Forczyk, 2013, 21).

However, diesel engines in tanks provided superior power, speed, and mobility to the vehicle. The T-34 of the Soviets used a diesel engine and showed great strategic and tactical mobility. While the Tigers, Panthers, and Elefants (Ferdinands) of Hitler's Citadel offensive proved devastating in combat with T-34s, KV-Is, KV-IIs, and various Lend-Lease tanks, they simply lumbered along too slowly to close the "pincers" of Citadel's encircling movement in the time allotted.

A Disabled T-34

Their slow strategic speed also enabled the Soviets to move numerous reinforcements into place to impede or block each arm of the offensive. Faster tanks might well have moved rapidly enough to thrust deeper into the salient's base before all of the Stavka's reserve armies could deploy to halt them. At the very least, diesel Panthers, Tigers, and Elefants would have permitted a more extensive pincer movement, increasing the chance of Hitler green-lighting further offensive operations.

While the Germans opened World War II – and, indeed, their actions in Russia during Operation Barbarossa – with "Blitzkrieg" tactics, these worked chiefly due to the nearly static tactics and strategy of their opponents. Though the Panzers represented formidable fighting machines, their mobility began and ended at a very low level. Their successful maneuvering in the early phases of the struggle only happened because the mobility of their adversaries proved even poorer. In effect, the Germans enjoyed initial luck in their enemies compensating for glaring flaws in their weapon systems.

The French in 1940 had tanks as lethal to the German tanks of their era as the Wehrmacht's own Tigers and Panthers later proved to T-35s and M4 Shermans. However, they remained hamstrung at the operational level due to the rarity of radios, leading to each tank fighting in isolation and thus succumbing to coordinated "packs" of weaker but better coordinated German armor. In other cases, the panzers simply bypassed the French tanks and allowed Luftwaffe air strikes to deal with them.

In the Soviet Union of 1941, Stalin ordered his men to hold position regardless of circumstances, making them easy prey for German encirclement and capture. These successes, in fact, probably tricked the Germans into believing their mobility surpassed that of all possible opponents. Kursk amply proved this view incorrect.

However, instead of focusing on improving their current tank models and then building them in large numbers, the Third Reich dissipated its remaining productive energy on bizarre experiments with a series of super-heavy tanks, such as the Panzer VIII Maus. This 287-ton monstrosity had a maximum speed of 12 mph and an off-road range of just 39 miles. The Germans built only two, neither of which saw action.

The Battle of Kursk, in effect, prompted the Germans to embrace the mobility problems of their armor design and exaggerate them to the point of caricature, while the Soviets created the upgraded T-34/85 on the same basic chassis and then built tens of thousands of these highly mobile tanks. Kursk's aftermath made the Wehrmacht cling to its weaknesses and the Red Army cleave to its strengths. Unsurprisingly, the Red Army won. This outcome can be said to be the main consequence of Operation Citadel.

Online Resources

Other World War II titles by Charles River Editors

Other titles about the Battle of Kursk on Amazon

Bibliography

Forczyk, Robert. Kursk 1943: The Northern Front. Botley, 2014.

Forczyk, Robert. Tank Warfare on the Eastern Front 1941-1942: Schwerpunkt. Barnsley, 2013.

Fowler, Will. Kursk: The Vital 24 Hours. London, 2005.

Frankson, Anders and Niklas Zetterling. Kursk 1943: A Statistical Analysis. Abingdon, 2004.

Healy, Mark. Kursk 1943: The Tide Turns in the East. London, 1992.

Kershaw, Ian. Hitler. New York, 2009.

Kurowski, Franz and David Johnston (translator). Panzer Aces. New York, 2002.

Lochmann, Franz-Wilhelm, Richard Freiherr von Rosen, Alfred Rubbel. The Combat   History of German Tiger Tank Battalion 503 in World War II. Mechanicsburg, 2008.

Munch, Karlheinz. The Combat History of German Heavy Anti-Tank Unit 653 in World War II.   Mechanicsburg, 2005.

Newton, Steven H. Kursk: the German View. Cambridge, 2002.

Nipe, George M. Decision in the Ukraine: German Panzer Operations on the Eastern Front, Summer 1943. Mechanicsburg, 2012.

Raus, Erhard. Panzer Operations: The Eastern Front Memoir of General Raus, 1941-1945. Boston, 2005.

Showalter, Dennis E. Armor and Blood: The Battle of Kursk. New York, 2013.

Zamulin, Valeriy. Demolishing the Myth: The Tank Battle at Prokhorovka, Kursk 1943: An Operational Narrative. Solihull, 2010.

CPSIA information can be obtained
at www.ICGtesting.com
Printed in the USA
LVOW13s1743050218
565344LV00045B/2614/P